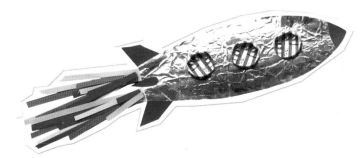

BLAST OFF!
THE SUN

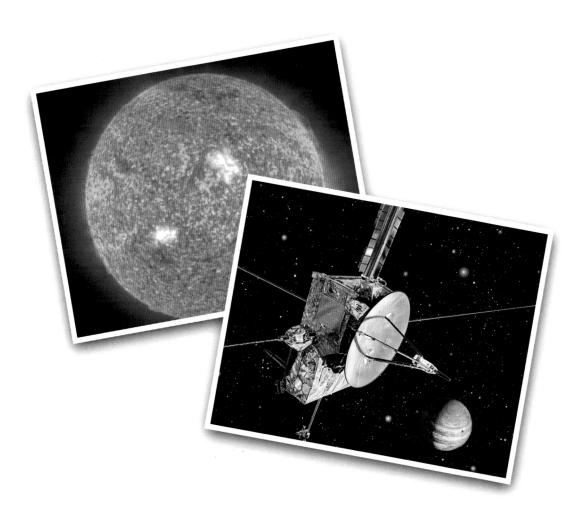

Helen and David Orme

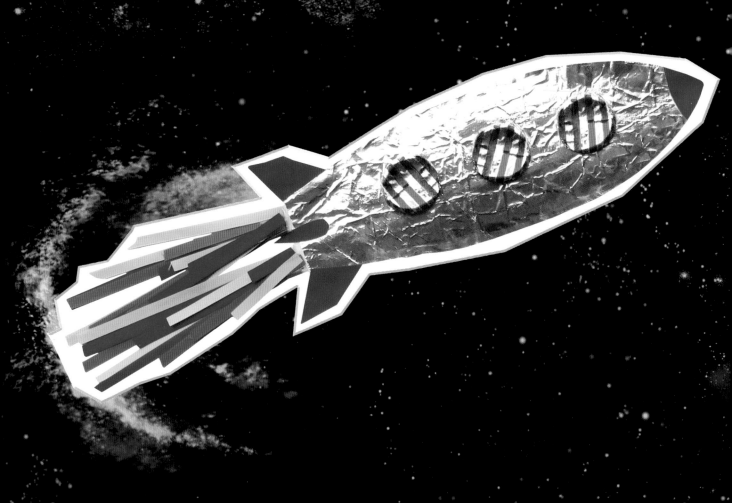

North American edition copyright © ticktock Entertainment Ltd 2009
First published in North America in 2009 by ticktock Media Ltd.,
The Old Sawmill, 103 Goods Station Road
Tunbridge Wells, Kent, TN1 2DP, U.K.

ticktock project editor: Julia Adams
ticktock project designer: Emma Randall

We would like to thank: Sandra Voss, Tim Bones, James Powell,
Indexing Specialists (U.K.) Ltd.

ISBN-13: 978-1-84898-155-3 pbk

Printed in China
9 8 7 6 5 4 3 2 1

All rights reserved. No part of this publication may be reproduced, copied, stored in a retrieval system, or transmitted in any form or
by any means electronic, mechanical, photocopying, recording, or otherwise without prior written permission of the copyright owner.

Picture credits (t=top; b=bottom; c=center; l=left; r=right; bg=background):
Art Directors: 20. Corbis: 21tr. NASA: 1all, 6bl, 7br, 8tl, 10, 11bl, 12br, 17bc, 22bl, 23 all. Science Photo Library: 4/5bg
(original), 5tr, 9tr, 9c, 18. Shutterstock: front cover, 2/3bg, 7bl, 13 all, 19 all, 22tr, 24bg. ticktock picture archive: 6/7bg, 7tl, 8br,
10/11, 11tr, 12tl, 14, 15 all, 16, 17tr, 21bl, 14/15bg, 18/19bg, 22/23bg.

Every effort has been made to trace the copyright holders, and we apologize in advance for any unintentional omissions.
We would be pleased to insert the appropriate acknowledgments in any subsequent edition of this publication.

Contents

The Sun in the Solar System . . 4–5

Sun Facts 6–7

The Birth of the Sun 8–9

The Sun's Life 10–11

Sunspots and Flares 12–13

Eclipses 14–15

Winds and Rays 16–17

What Can We See? 18–19

The Sun in History 20–21

Missions to the Sun 22–23

Glossary and Index 24

The Sun in the Solar System

The Sun is the center of our **solar system**. Without it, the solar system would not exist! All the planets, moons, and **asteroids** in our solar system **orbit** around it.

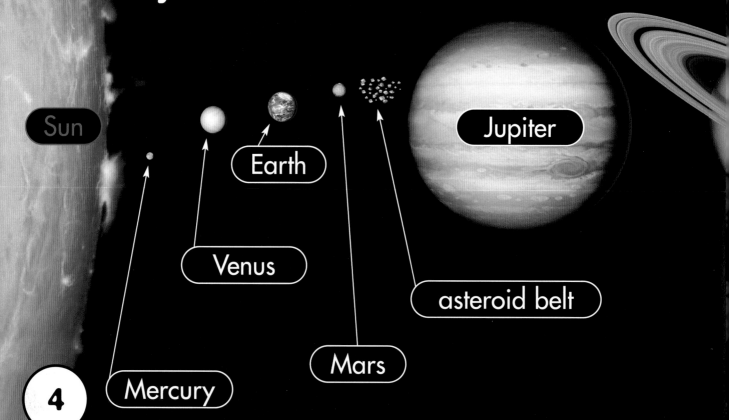

Sun

Earth

Venus

Jupiter

asteroid belt

Mars

Mercury

The Sun is a star. This means it creates light and heat. It is the closest star to Earth. You can see thousands of other stars in the sky. They are all much farther away.

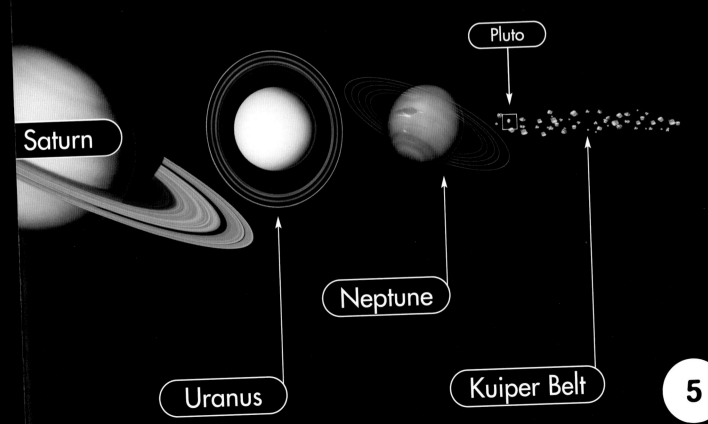

Pluto

Saturn

Neptune

Uranus

Kuiper Belt

Sun Facts

The Sun is the most important object in the **solar system**. It gives all the planets heat and light. Without the Sun, life would not be possible on Earth.

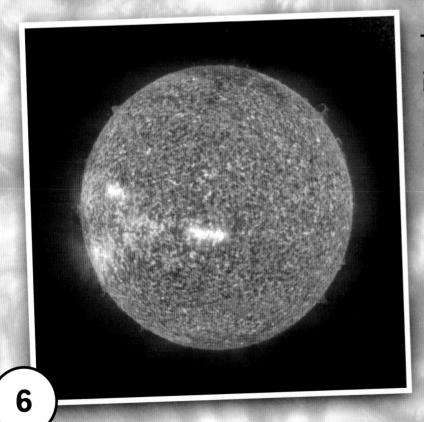

The center of the Sun is mostly made of **hydrogen gas**. This gas turns into **helium gas**. When this happens, the Sun creates a lot of heat and light.

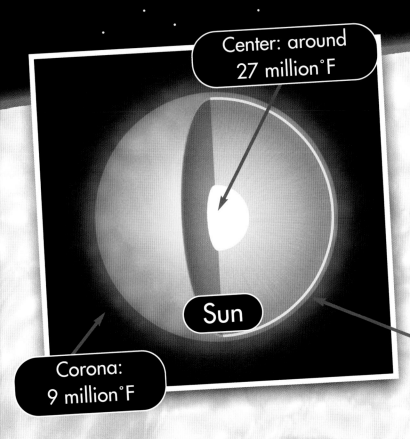

Center: around 27 million°F

Sun

Corona: 9 million°F

Outer layer: 9,932°F

The Sun is very, very hot. There is nothing we can compare the temperature with on Earth. We can't even imagine how hot the Sun is!

This picture shows how big the Sun is compared to Earth. The Sun looks small from Earth because it is so far away.

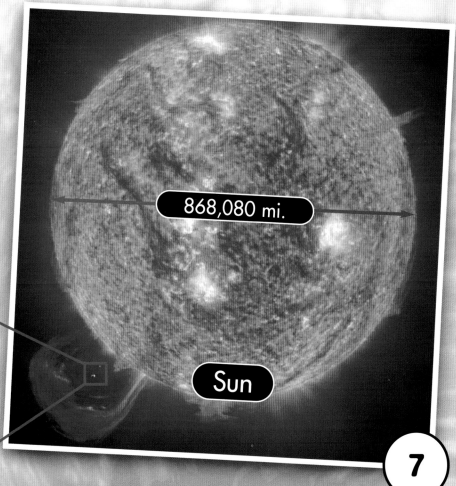

868,080 mi.

Sun

7,909 mi.

Earth

The Birth of the Sun

The Sun began its life billions of years ago. Before the Sun was there, our **solar system** did not exist!

Billions of years ago, a great cloud of gas and dust began to form.

This cloud of gas began to form a spinning disk with a huge bulge in the middle. The disk began spinning faster and faster.

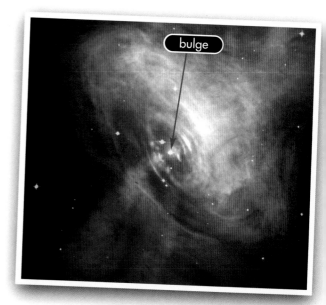

bulge

The huge bulge kept heating up until it started turning **hydrogen gas** into **helium gas**.

bulge

bulge

The great bulge was turning into the Sun. At the same time, the planets were formed from the rest of the gassy disk.

The Sun's Life

The Sun is around 4½ billion years old! Like people, animals, and planets, it was born, will have a lifetime, and then it will die.

The Sun is made of **hydrogen gas**. The hydrogen gas is turning into **helium gas**. This creates a lot of heat.

Almost half of the hydrogen the Sun is made of has now turned into helium. It will take around 5 billion years for all the hydrogen to be used up.

When all the hydrogen has been turned into helium, the Sun will start to grow bigger. It will grow up to 100 times its original size! Then it will be called a Red Giant.

Sun

Red Giant

White Dwarf

Then the Sun's outer layers will start turning into a cloud of gas. The gas will slowly disappear and leave he Sun's center. The Sun will start to cool down, although this will take millions of years. Stars like this are called White Dwarfs.

Sunspots and Flares

The Sun sometimes has spots on its outer layer. These are places where the temperature is lower.

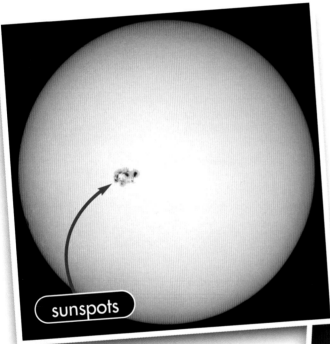

sunspots

Sunspots are not always in the same place on the Sun. Scientists have found out that every 11 years, the Sun has more sunspots than usual.

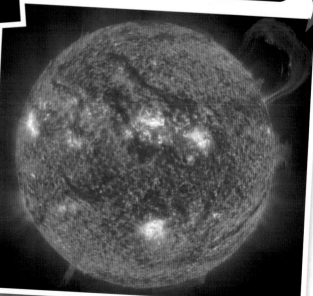

flare

Sometimes there are huge explosions on the Sun. This means that extremely hot **particles** of the Sun are hurled into space. They are called flares.

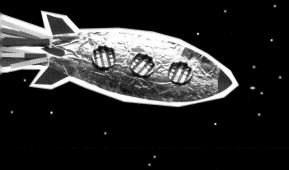

The hot particles from the Sun can reach Earth in a few days. When they hit Earth's **atmosphere**, the sky lights up in different colors.

Earth

This photograph shows what happens when hot particles from the Sun reach Earth's atmosphere in the north. This is called Aurora Borealis, or Northern Lights.

This is a photograph of the Aurora Australis, or Southern Lights. You can see them when the Sun's hot particles reach Earth's atmosphere in the south.

Earth

Eclipses

Sometimes our moon
moves between Earth and the Sun.
When this happens, all or part of the Sun
is covered over. This is called an eclipse.

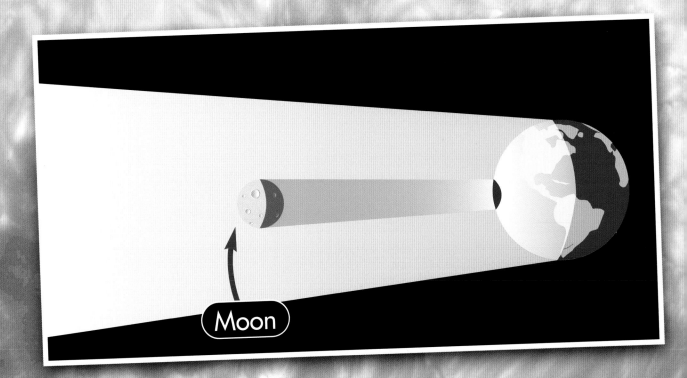

Moon

This picture shows what happens when the
Moon moves between the Sun and Earth.
The shadow marks the spot on Earth where you
can see the Moon blocking out the Sun entirely.
This is called a total eclipse.

Moon covering part of the Sun

This is a **partial** eclipse of the Sun. It means that only a part of the Sun is covered by the Moon.

Sun

Moon covering the Sun

This is a total eclipse of the Sun. It doesn't happen very often. When it happens, it is possible to see the glowing gas (corona) that is around the Sun.

glowing Corona

Winds and Rays

The Sun doesn't just create heat and light. All types of **rays** come from the Sun. Some of them are dangerous to all life on Earth.

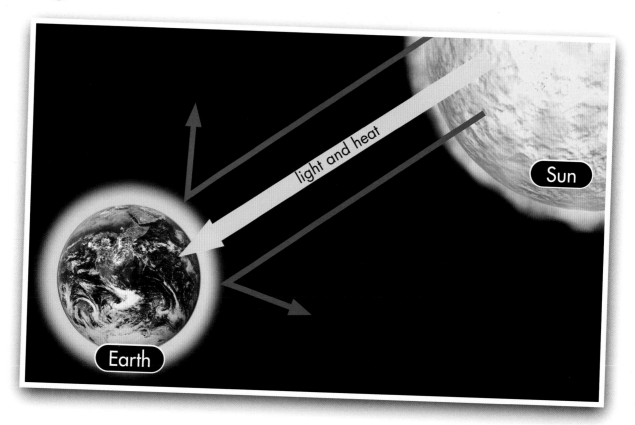

light and heat

Sun

Earth

This picture shows the heat and light from the Sun reaching Earth. The red arrows show the dangerous rays. The **atmosphere** helps stop dangerous rays from coming through to Earth.

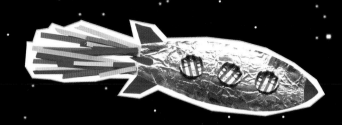

Particles pour out of the Sun at high speed. This is called the solar wind. It travels at more than ½ million mi. per hour!

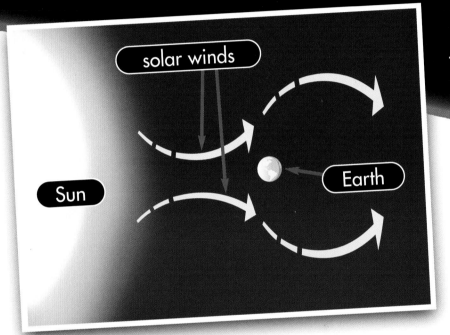

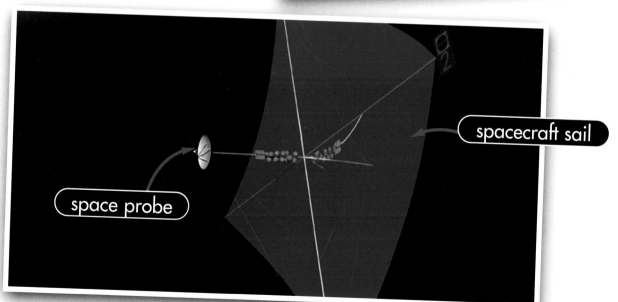

Some scientists think the solar wind could be used to push spacecraft along, like sailing ships!

What Can We See?

Trying to look at the Sun through a telescope can burn your eyes very badly. This is why watching the Sun is very difficult.

Sun

telescope

projection of the Sun

Early **astronomers** used a telescope to project a picture of the Sun onto a piece of paper. They set up the telescope so that the Sun shone through it. Then they held a piece of paper in front of the telescope, like in this photo.

Today, scientists use special filters for telescopes. They also study pictures that spacecraft send back.

Warning
NEVER look directly at the Sun. It can blind you!

The Sun has a huge effect on life on Earth. Without it, humans, animals, and plants could not exist. Plants need sunlight to grow, and animals and humans need plants like vegetables and fruit to live.

The Sun makes our skin turn darker. But the Sun can harm our skin and burn it. This is why we have to protect our skin with clothes or sunblock.

The Sun in History

For thousands of years, people have worshiped the Sun. It could make their crops grow, but it could also dry up their fields. The Sun was important and powerful.

In ancient Egypt, people worshiped a Sun god called Ra. He was the king of the gods. In pictures, Ra has a human body, the head of a hawk, and a sun headdress.

The Greeks and Romans called their Sun god Helios. They believed he crossed the sky in a flaming **chariot**.

In Hinduism, people have believed in a Sun god for thousands of years. He is called Surya, and he rides a chariot with seven horses.

Missions to the Sun

Scientists study the different rays coming from the Sun. This helps them understand how it affects Earth.

Our **atmosphere** makes it very difficult to study the Sun. This is because it filters out many of the Sun's rays. The best way to study the Sun is to send **space probes** and **satellites** into space.

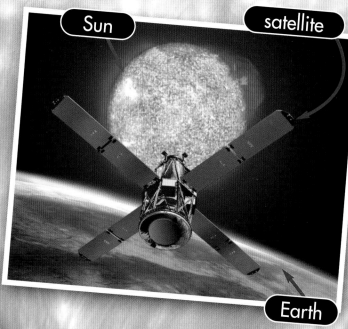

Sun
satellite
Earth

Ulysses

This space probe is called Ulysses. It was launched in 1990 and reached the Sun in 1994. It has been sending back information about the Sun's outer layer and solar winds ever since.

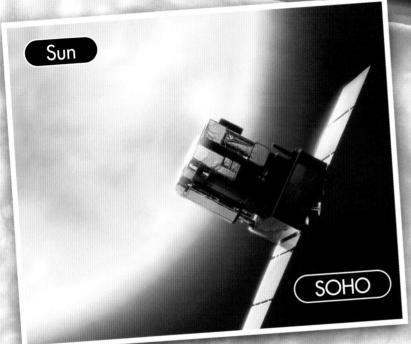

Sun

SOHO

This is the space probe SOHO (**So**lar and **H**eliospheric **O**bservatory). SOHO has been studying the Sun since 1995.

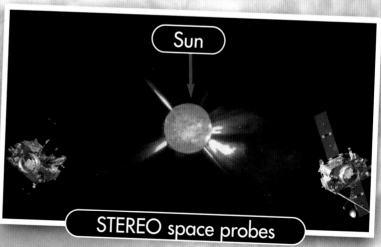

Sun

STEREO space probes

NASA is planning a new mission called STEREO (**S**olar **TE**rrestrial **RE**lations **O**bservatory). Two space probes will be sent to the Sun. They will take 3-D pictures of the Sun's flares.

Glossary

Asteroids Rocky objects that orbit the Sun. Most asteroids orbit the Sun between Mars and Jupiter.

Astronomers People who study space, often using telescopes.

Atmosphere The gases that surround a star, planet, or moon.

Chariot A cart that is drawn by horses.

Helium gas A gas that is lighter than air. We use helium to fill balloons!

Hydrogen gas A very light gas. It is extremely explosive.

NASA (short for National Aeronautics and Space Administration) An American group of scientists and astronauts who research space.

Orbit The path planets or other objects take around the Sun, or satellites take around planets.

Partial When something is not complete.

Particles Tiny amounts or very small pieces of something.

Rays Beams of light and warmth. Some rays are dangerous because they are very harmful to life on Earth.

Satellites Moons or man-made objects that are in orbit around a planet.

Solar system The Sun and everything that is in orbit around it.

Space probe A spacecraft sent from Earth to explore the solar system. It can collect samples and take pictures.

Index

astronomers 18

atmosphere 16, 22

eclipses 14–5

flares 12–13, 23

gods 20–1

helium gas 6, 9–11

history 20–1

hydrogen gas 6, 9–11

life of the Sun 10–11

missions 22–3

NASA 22

Northern Lights 13

rays 16, 22

Red Giants 11

solar system 4–6, 8

solar winds 17, 22

Southern Lights 13

space probes 22–3

stars 5

sunspots 12

telescopes 18

temperature 7

White Dwarfs 11

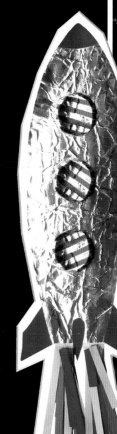